Real Estate is for Everyone!

Dominic Lyon

ISBN: 979-8-85-204282-8

DEDICATION

To my lifelong editor. Thank you, Mom!

TABLE OF CONTENTS

INTRODUCTION AND THE IMPORTANCE OF
REAL ESTATE IN WEALTH CREATION

Welcome to the fascinating world of real estate investment! In this book, we will embark on a journey that challenges conventional beliefs and empowers you to realize that real estate is not an exclusive domain reserved solely for the privileged few. Instead, it is an accessible avenue for wealth creation available to individuals from all walks of life. By delving into the fundamentals of real estate and debunking common misconceptions, we aim to equip you with the knowledge and confidence to embark on your own successful real estate investment journey.

The Power of Real Estate:

Real estate, throughout history, has proven to be a formidable wealth-building vehicle. It holds a unique position in the financial landscape, offering both stability and potential for significant returns. The allure of tangible assets, the ability to generate passive income, and the potential for appreciation are just a few reasons why real estate has stood the test of time as a reliable means of wealth creation. Whether considering residential properties, commercial spaces, or even raw land, real estate holds inherent value and the capacity to generate long-term financial prosperity.

Unfortunately, real estate investment has often been shrouded in mystery, perpetuating misconceptions that have discouraged many from exploring this promising field. Let us address some of these fallacies head-on:

Myth: Real estate is <u>only for the wealthy</u>.

<u>Reality</u>: While it is true that some real estate investments require significant capital, there are numerous entry points available to individuals with varying financial means. Creative financing options, partnerships, and leveraging resources can make real estate accessible to a wide range of investors.

In fact, real estate offers diverse investment opportunities tailored to different budgets and risk tolerances. For instance, you can begin by investing in residential properties such as single-family homes or condominiums. These properties often have lower price points compared to commercial real estate, making them more affordable for entry-level investors. Moreover, real estate investment trusts (REITs) offer an avenue for individuals to invest in real estate without having to directly own properties, allowing for more modest investments.

Myth: Real estate investment is <u>too complex</u> and <u>time-consuming</u>.

<u>Reality</u>: While real estate does require knowledge and effort, it does not have to be an overwhelming or burdensome undertaking. With the right strategies, systems, and guidance, investing in real estate can be a manageable and rewarding endeavor.

Education and understanding the fundamentals of real estate are crucial to navigate the complexities of the market. By equipping yourself with the necessary knowledge, you can make educated decisions and minimize potential pitfalls. Additionally, leveraging technology and utilizing various tools available can simplify processes and save time. Real estate investment can be as hands-on or hands-off as you desire, allowing you to tailor your approach based on your preferences and available resources.

Myth: Real estate investment is <u>too risky</u>.

<u>Reality</u>: Real estate involves innate risks. However, with a thorough understanding of the market, careful due diligence, and a proactive approach to risk management, it is possible to mitigate and navigate these risks effectively.

Real estate investment requires a comprehensive analysis of factors such as location, property conditions, financial feasibility, and market condition. Conducting due diligence, that is, having property inspections, doing market research and financial analyses, helps to identify potential risks and make informed investment decisions. In addition, diversifying your real estate portfolio with different types of properties and locations will assist with mitigation of risk by increasing exposure.

Myth: Real estate investment is a <u>gamble</u>.

<u>Reality</u>: Unlike speculative ventures, real estate investment allows for calculated decisions based on market analysis, property evaluation, and strategic planning. By employing sound investment principles and adopting a long-term perspective, you can minimize the element of chance and maximize your success.

Successful real estate investors rely on thorough research and analysis to identify properties with strong potential for appreciation and cash flow. By understanding market trends, studying comparable sales, and conducting financial analyses, you can make <u>data-driven decisions</u>. Real estate also benefits from the principle of <u>leverage</u>, where financing is used to amplify returns and increase purchasing power, further reducing the element of chance.

In the pages that follow, we will dismantle these misconceptions, providing you with a solid foundation in real estate investment. By exploring the diverse avenues within this realm and sharing practical strategies, you will be empowered to embark on your own path towards financial independence and wealth creation. Remember, real estate is <u>not an elusive dream</u>, attainable only by a select few; it is an opportunity <u>open to everyone</u> willing to <u>learn, adapt, and take action.</u>

So, let us challenge the status quo together and discover how real estate truly <u>is</u> for everyone! In the next chapter, we will probe into the fundamentals of real estate, unraveling the different types of properties and understanding key terminology and concepts. Join us as we lay the groundwork for your real estate journey!

1 EXPLORING THE DIFFERENT TYPES OF REAL ESTATE

As we begin our journey into the world of real estate, we must gain a comprehensive understanding of the various types of properties that form the backbone of this dynamic industry. This chapter will explore the diverse components within real estate, from residential homes to commercial spaces, and even the possibilities presented by raw land. By investigating the nuances of each category, we will lay the groundwork for your real estate investment endeavors.

Residential Real Estate:

Residential real estate encompasses properties intended for private living, catering to individuals, families, or households. This segment will consider single-family homes, townhouses, condominiums, duplexes, and apartment buildings. Residential properties offer opportunities for both short-term gains, through appreciation and rental income, and long-term wealth accumulation through property ownership.

Single-family homes are the primary form of residential properties, offering individuals a sense of ownership and privacy that is often sought in the real estate market. Townhouses show a balance

1

between single-family homes and condominiums, often featuring shared walls and amenities. Condominiums, (condos), provide ownership of individual units within a larger building or complex, with shared ownership of common areas. Duplexes, triplexes, and fourplexes allow for multiple units within a single structure, enabling owners to, perhaps, live in one unit while renting out the others. Apartment buildings, on the other hand, are designed for multiple tenants, offering higher profits through rental income and scalability.

Residential real estate investments can provide stable cash flow through rental income, tax advantages through deductions, and the potential for property appreciation. These properties often appeal to investors seeking a more hands-on approach to real estate management or those looking for a place to call home while enjoying the benefits of real estate ownership.

Commercial Real Estate:

Commercial real estate involves properties that are used for business or investment purposes. It encompasses a vast spectrum, including office buildings, retail spaces, industrial warehouses, hotels, and multifamily complexes. Commercial properties provide unique investment prospects, as they often generate higher rental income and offer potential for significant capital appreciation. Additionally, lease agreements with commercial tenants can provide stability and long-term cash flow.

Office buildings are designed to accommodate businesses, offering spaces for various industries and professions. Retail spaces encompass a variety of commercial properties such as shopping centers, strip malls, and standalone storefronts, providing premises dedicated for businesses operating within the retail sector. Industrial warehouses and manufacturing facilities are essential for logistics, storage, and production purposes. Hotels and hospitality properties are tailored for temporary accommodation and can range from small boutique establishments to large resorts. Multifamily complexes are residential properties designed for multiple tenants, such as apartment complexes or condominium buildings.

Investing in commercial real estate requires a thorough understanding of market dynamics, tenant demands, and the specific needs of different industries. The lease terms of commercial properties are generally longer than those of residential properties and have higher capital requirements. However, they can provide attractive returns, especially in prime locations with high demand.

Raw Land and Development:

Raw land represents untapped potential within the real estate sphere. This category encompasses vacant lots, undeveloped parcels, and agricultural tracts. Investing in raw land offers opportunities for development, such as constructing residential or commercial properties, creating subdivisions, or engaging in land speculation. Raw land investments require vision, market analysis, and an understanding of zoning and regulatory factors.

Raw land can be an intriguing investment option for those willing to take on more significant risks and actively participate in the development process. It requires thorough research to assess the property's potential, including factors such as location, accessibility, zoning regulations, and future growth prospects. Raw land investments often involve longer holding periods and require additional due diligence to ensure feasibility and to mitigate potential obstacles.

Understanding Key Terminology and Concepts:

Real estate, like any industry, has its own lexicon of terms and concepts. Familiarizing yourself with these key terms will not only enhance your understanding but also enable effective communication within the real estate realm. Let's explore some fundamental terminology:

- **Equity:** The difference between the market value of a property and the outstanding mortgage balance. It represents the owner's ownership interest in the property.
- **Appreciation:** The increase in the value of a property over time, typically influenced by market conditions, demand, and improvements made to the property.
- **Cash Flow:** The net income generated from a real estate investment after deducting expenses such as mortgage payments, property taxes, insurance, maintenance, and vacancies.
- **Capitalization Rate (Cap Rate):** A metric used to assess the potential return on investment for a property. It is calculated by dividing the net operating income by the property's purchase price or value.
- **Leverage:** The use of borrowed funds, such as a mortgage or loan, to finance an investment. Leverage has the potential to amplify returns, but it also carries an elevated level of risk.

These terms provide the beginning foundation for understanding the financial aspects of real estate investment. Mastering these concepts will enable you to evaluate opportunities, analyze potential risks, and make informed decisions. Learning real estate investment concepts such as equity, appreciation, cash flow, capitalization rate, and leverage is crucial for building a strong foundation in real estate investing. Here are some effective ways to learn and understand these concepts:

1. **Real Estate Education Courses and Workshops:**

    Consider enrolling in real estate education courses or workshops offered by reputable institutions, community colleges, or online platforms.

These courses often cover fundamental concepts and provide practical examples to help you grasp the concepts of equity, appreciation, cash flow, capitalization rate, and leverage. Look for courses specifically tailored to real estate investing or general real estate principles.

2. **Books and Publications:**

   Explore books, publications, and resources dedicated to real estate investing. There are numerous books written by industry experts that explain these concepts in a clear and accessible manner. Look for books that cover the fundamentals of real estate investing or focus specifically on the concepts you want to learn. Some recommended titles include "The ABCs of Real Estate Investing" by Ken McElroy, "Rich Dad Poor Dad" by Robert Kiyosaki, and "The Millionaire Real Estate Investor" by Gary Keller.

3. **Online Resources and Blogs:**

   Utilize online resources and blogs dedicated to real estate investing. There are several reputable websites and blogs that provide educational content, articles, and guides on various real estate investment concepts. Look for resources that explain equity, appreciation, cash flow, capitalization rate, and leverage in simple terms and provide practical examples. BiggerPockets, Investopedia, and The Balance are popular websites that cover a wide range of real estate topics.

4. **Real Estate Investment Groups and Forums:**

   Join real estate investment groups or forums where experienced investors and enthusiasts share their knowledge and experiences. Participating in discussions, asking questions, and seeking advice from seasoned investors can be an invaluable way to learn about equity, appreciation, cash flow, capitalization rate, and leverage. Networking with other investors can also provide opportunities to gain practical insights and learn from real-world experiences.

5. **Mentors and Real Estate Professionals:**

Seek guidance from mentors and real estate professionals who have expertise in the concepts you want to learn. Engage with experienced individuals who can provide personalized guidance and advice suited to your specific needs. Consider reaching out to local real estate agents, property managers, or real estate investment advisors who can share their knowledge and offer guidance on equity, appreciation, cash flow, capitalization rate, and leverage.

6. **Webinars and Podcasts:**

Attend webinars or listen to real estate podcasts that focus on educating listeners about real estate investment concepts. Many industry experts and experienced investors host webinars and podcasts where they discuss various aspects of real estate investing, including equity, appreciation, cash flow, capitalization rate, and leverage. These platforms often provide real-life examples and case studies to help you understand these concepts in practical terms.

Remember, learning real estate investment concepts takes time and continuous effort. It is necessary to combine theoretical knowledge with practical application through hands-on experience and learning from mistakes. As you progress on your real estate investment journey, consider applying these concepts in real-life scenarios and continuously seeking opportunities to expand your knowledge and understanding.

Real Estate in a Diversified Investment Portfolio:

Real estate holds a crucial position within a diversified investment portfolio, offering stability, income generation, and potential capital appreciation. By incorporating real estate into your investment strategy, you can mitigate risks and enhance overall portfolio performance. Here are some reasons why real estate is a valuable component of a diversified portfolio:

- **Asset Diversification:** Real estate provides an opportunity to diversify investments beyond traditional stocks, bonds, and mutual funds, reducing vulnerability to market fluctuations and enhancing portfolio resilience.
- **Income Generation:** Rental income from real estate properties can provide a consistent cash flow stream, offering a hedge against economic downturns and supplementing other investment returns.
- **Inflation Hedge:** Real estate investments have historically demonstrated the potential to outpace inflation, as property values and rental income tend to rise with the cost of living.
- **Tangible Asset:** Real estate represents a tangible, physical asset that can provide a sense of security and control. Unlike stocks or bonds, real estate offers a physical presence and the potential for personal use or enjoyment.
- **Portfolio Stability:** Real estate investments can contribute to portfolio stability due to their comparatively lower volatility, especially when combined with other asset classes with varying risk profiles.

By including real estate in your investment portfolio, you can create a balanced approach that accounts for both long-term growth and income generation, leading to increased wealth accumulation and financial security.

In this chapter, we have laid the foundation of our journey by exploring the different types of real estate, understanding key terminology and concepts, and recognizing the significance of real estate in a diversified investment portfolio. Armed with this knowledge, you are now equipped to embark on a deeper exploration of the real estate world. In the following chapters, we will dig further into the intricacies of real estate property evaluation, financing options, risk management, and investment strategies. So, let us continue our exploration to discover the vast opportunities that real estate presents on the path to financial prosperity.

2 OVERCOMING BARRIERS TO ENTRY

One of the most persistent misconceptions surrounding real estate investment is that it is an exclusive domain reserved only for the wealthy. In this chapter, we aim to dispel this myth and showcase that real estate is, indeed, an avenue <u>accessible to individuals from all financial backgrounds</u>. By understanding the strategies, options, and opportunities available, aspiring investors can overcome the perceived barriers and embark on their own real estate investment journey.

Real estate investment is not solely reserved for those with substantial capital. In fact, there are numerous ways to enter the real estate market regardless of your financial means. By shifting our perspective and embracing creative strategies, we can level the playing field and open doors to real estate opportunities for everyone.

Traditional Financing:

Traditional financing options provide a common pathway for individuals to acquire properties. These include:

- **Conventional Mortgages:** Traditional bank loans that allow individuals to purchase properties with a down payment and regular mortgage payments. These loans often come with fixed or adjustable interest rates and repayment terms typically ranging from 15 to 30 years.

- **Government-Backed Loans:** Programs such as FHA loans, VA loans, and USDA loans that offer flexible qualification requirements and lower down payment options. These loan programs are designed to help individuals with limited resources or specific eligibility criteria, such as veterans or those purchasing properties in rural areas.

Seller Financing:

Seller financing offers an alternative approach where the seller assists the buyer in securing the necessary financing. Two common forms of seller financing are:

- **Lease-to-Own Agreements:** A seller agrees to lease the property to the buyer with an option to purchase at a predetermined price and within a specified timeframe. This arrangement allows aspiring investors to build equity and improve their financial situation while enjoying the benefits of living in the property.
- **Seller-Carryback Financing:** The seller acts as the lender, providing a loan to the buyer, eliminating the need for traditional financing. This approach can be advantageous for individuals who may face challenges obtaining a bank loan but have established a rapport with the seller.

Partnerships and Joint Ventures:

Pooling resources through partnerships and joint ventures can provide opportunities for individuals to enter the real estate market. Some strategies include:

- **Pooling Resources:** Partnering with other investors to combine financial resources and expertise, sharing the risks and rewards of real estate investments. This collaborative approach allows individuals to access larger-scale projects that may be beyond their individual capacity.

- **Equity Partnerships:** Working with investors who provide the necessary capital in exchange for a share of ownership and potential profits. This arrangement enables individuals to leverage the financial resources of others while benefiting from their experience and industry knowledge.

Creative Strategies:

In addition to traditional financing and partnerships, creative strategies can help individuals overcome barriers to entry. Some notable approaches include:

- **Wholesaling:** Finding off-market properties at a discounted price and assigning the contract to another buyer for a fee. Wholesaling requires a keen eye for market opportunities and strong negotiation skills.
- **Real Estate Investment Trusts (REITs):** Investing in publicly traded REITs that allow individuals to own shares of real estate portfolios without directly owning properties. REITs provide diversification, professional management, and the potential for steady income through dividends.

Building a solid financial foundation is essential for successful real estate investment. Here are key steps to consider:

- **Establishing Financial Goals:** Define short-term and long-term financial objectives related to real estate investment, such as generating passive income, achieving capital appreciation, or building a retirement fund. Setting clear goals will guide your investment decisions.
- **Budgeting and Saving:** Create a comprehensive budget to control expenses and allocate funds towards savings and investment. Building an emergency fund is imperative in

handling unexpected expenses or vacancies without risking your real estate investments.

- **Improving Creditworthiness:** Pay bills on time, reduce debt, and maintain a good credit score to enhance eligibility for financing options and secure favorable loan terms. A strong credit history opens doors to more attractive financing options and lower interest rates.

- **Education and Skill Development:** Invest in real estate education through books, courses, seminars, and networking opportunities to acquire knowledge and develop essential skills. Continuous learning will empower you to make informed decisions and navigate the complexities of the real estate market.

In this chapter, we have debunked the myth that real estate investment is exclusively for the wealthy. By exploring creative financing options, such as traditional mortgages, seller financing, partnerships, and joint ventures, we have demonstrated that there are pathways for individuals with varying financial means to enter the real estate market. Additionally, we have emphasized the importance of building a solid financial foundation through budgeting, saving, improving creditworthiness, and investing in education. Armed with this knowledge, you are now equipped to overcome the barriers to entry and begin your real estate investment journey. In the upcoming chapters, we will delve further into selecting the right investment strategy, evaluating opportunities, and managing your real estate investments effectively.

3 CHOOSING THE RIGHT INVESTMENT STRATEGY

Selecting the right investment strategy is crucial when venturing into the world of real estate. In this chapter, we will explore the importance of aligning your investment approach with your personal goals and risk tolerance. By understanding your unique objectives and comfort level, you can make informed decisions that pave the way for a successful and fulfilling real estate investment journey.

To select the optimal investment strategy, it is essential to clearly define your financial objectives. Consider the following:

- **Generating Passive Income:** If your primary goal is to generate consistent cash flow, rental properties can be an attractive option. By becoming a landlord and renting out residential or commercial properties, you can receive regular rental payments, which can supplement your income and provide financial stability.
- **Achieving Long-Term Capital Appreciation:** Some investors seek to build wealth over the long term through property appreciation. Investing in properties in growing areas with the potential for value appreciation can be a viable strategy for achieving capital gains over time.

- **Building a Diverse Investment Portfolio:** Real estate can be an excellent addition to a diversified investment portfolio. By including real estate as a component of your investment portfolio, you will mitigate risk and capitalize on the potential advantages that this asset class offers.
- **Securing a Retirement Fund:** Real estate investments can play a significant role in building a retirement fund. Rental properties, for example, can provide a steady stream of income during retirement, allowing you to enjoy financial independence.

It is crucial to assess your time horizons and desired investment outcomes to align your strategy with your goals. Real estate investments can vary in terms of their holding periods and expected returns. Some investments may offer quick returns, while others may require a longer-term commitment to achieve optimal results. Consider whether you are looking for short-term gains or are willing to invest for a more extended period to maximize your returns.

Understanding and assessing your personal comfort level with risk and volatility is a fundamental step in developing a successful real estate investment strategy. Real estate, like any investment, comes with inherent risks and the potential for volatility. By understanding your risk tolerance, you can accordingly align your investment approach with your own financial goals, time horizon, and emotional resilience.

Risk tolerance refers to your ability and willingness to accept potential losses or fluctuations in investment value. It is influenced by factors such as your financial situation, investment experience, future goals, and personal preferences. Some individuals may be comfortable with higher levels of risk and volatility in pursuit of potentially higher returns, while others may prioritize stability and lower-risk investments.

Assessing your risk tolerance involves a combination of objective analysis and introspection. It is essential to objectively evaluate your financial circumstances, including your income, savings, and existing investment portfolio. Also consider additional personal factors, including your age, investment time frame, and overarching financial objectives. This analysis will provide you with a clearer understanding of how much risk you can afford to take.

Equally important is the introspective aspect of assessing your risk tolerance. Reflect on your emotional response to market fluctuations, your ability to handle uncertainty, and your long-term investment goals. It is crucial to find a balance between taking enough risk to achieve your financial objectives and avoiding excessive stress or anxiety.

Once you have a better understanding of your risk tolerance, you can choose an investment strategy that aligns with your comfort level. Real estate offers a range of investment options, from low-risk income-generating properties to higher-risk development projects or speculative investments. Consider diversifying your portfolio across different property types, locations, and investment strategies to spread risk and mitigate the impact of volatility.

Additionally, staying informed about market conditions and trends can help you make more informed decisions regarding risk management. Monitoring economic indicators, market reports, and industry insights will enable you to assess the potential risks and rewards associated with specific real estate investments. This knowledge will help you determine whether the potential returns justify the level of risk involved.

Remember that risk tolerance is not static and can evolve over time. As you gain experience and knowledge in real estate investing, your comfort level with risk may change. Regularly reassess your risk tolerance and adjust your investment strategy accordingly.

Ultimately, understanding your comfort level with risk and volatility is essential for selecting an investment strategy that aligns with your financial goals and emotional well-being. By being honest with yourself, conducting thorough analyses, and staying informed, you can navigate the dynamic world of real estate with confidence and maximize the potential of your investments. Factors to consider include:

- **Financial Stability:** Evaluate your financial situation and determine how much risk you can afford to take. If you have a stable income, significant savings, and a secure financial foundation, you may be more comfortable with higher-risk investments.
- **Investment Experience:** Your experience and knowledge of real estate investments will influence your risk tolerance. If you are a seasoned investor with a deep understanding of the market, you may be more willing to take on higher-risk strategies.
- **Emotional Resilience:** Consider your ability to handle market fluctuations and potential setbacks. Real estate investments can be subject to market volatility and unexpected challenges, and your emotional resilience will play a role in how you navigate these situations.

When choosing an investment strategy, it is important to balance the potential rewards with the associated risks. Higher-risk strategies often offer the possibility of greater returns but also carry a higher chance of loss. On the other hand, lower-risk strategies may offer more stability but potentially lower returns. Assess the potential returns against the risks involved and choose a strategy that aligns with your risk tolerance and investment goals.

Now that we have defined personal goals and assessed risk tolerance, let us explore different investment strategies in the real estate market:

Rental Properties

Engaging in rental property investment involves acquiring residential or commercial properties with the aim of generating income from rental payments. Some benefits of this strategy include consistent cash flow, long-term wealth accumulation through property appreciation, and potential tax advantages. Nevertheless, assuming the role of a landlord entails various responsibilities, including property management, tenant screening, and property maintenance.

Fix-and-Flip

The fix-and-flip strategy encompasses acquiring properties at a price below their market value, undertaking renovations or improvements, and subsequently selling them at a higher price to generate a profit. Executing this strategy necessitates a discerning perspective to identify the potential in properties, expertise in renovation and improvement techniques, and a profound understanding of market trends and dynamics. While it can be a potentially lucrative strategy, it also carries higher risks, such as unexpected renovation costs or difficulty selling the property.

Real Estate Investment Trusts (REITs)

REITs are publicly traded companies that allow individuals to own shares of diversified real estate portfolios. By investing in REITs, you can access real estate markets with lower capital requirements and benefit from liquidity and professional management. REITs offer the opportunity to invest in a range of property types, such as residential, commercial, or industrial, without the need for direct ownership and management.

Vacation Rentals and Short-Term Rentals

Renting out properties on a short-term basis through platforms like Airbnb or VRBO has become a popular investment strategy. This approach requires careful location analysis, property management skills, and understanding local regulations. By targeting popular tourist destinations or areas with high rental demand, you can potentially earn higher rental income compared to long-term rentals. Nonetheless, it is crucial to consider the <u>seasonality</u> of the rental market and the potential obstacles that may arise when managing properties intended for short-term rentals.

To make informed and strategic investment decisions, it is crucial to have a deep understanding of market conditions, trends, and their potential impact on your real estate ventures. The real estate market is dynamic and constantly evolving, influenced by various factors such as economic indicators, demographic shifts, and regulatory changes. Therefore, staying informed and conducting thorough market research is essential for success in this industry.

By monitoring market conditions, you can identify emerging opportunities, anticipate potential risks, and adjust your investment strategies accordingly. Understanding market trends allows you to assess the demand and supply dynamics, property values, and rental rates in specific areas or property types. This knowledge empowers you to make well-informed decisions regarding property acquisitions, financing options, and optimal timing for buying or selling.

To gain insights into market conditions, consider utilizing various sources of information. Stay updated with industry publications, real estate websites, and reports from reputable organizations. Local market reports and economic indicators can provide valuable data on job growth, population trends, and infrastructure developments, all of which can significantly impact the real estate market.

Additionally, networking and building relationships within the real estate community can provide you with firsthand information and local market expertise. Engage with fellow investors, real estate professionals, and local organizations to access insights, market analysis, and potential investment opportunities. By actively participating in industry events, seminars, and online forums, you can stay connected with the pulse of the market and gain valuable perspectives from experienced professionals.

Remember, understanding market conditions and trends is not a one-time endeavor. Continuously monitoring and analyzing market data will help you adapt your investment strategies and identify new avenues for growth. Be proactive in seeking knowledge, exploring different markets, and adapting to changing circumstances to maximize the potential of your real estate investments.

By providing yourself with this knowledge of market conditions and trends, you can make informed investment decisions that align with your goals and increase the likelihood of success in today's changeable world of real estate. Now, further consider the following:

Market Research

Conduct comprehensive market analyses to identify favorable locations, rental demand, vacancy rates, and potential growth areas. Understanding local economic factors, employment trends, infrastructure development, and demographic shifts can provide valuable insights for selecting the right investment strategy.

Real Estate Cycles

Real estate markets are cyclical, experiencing phases of expansion, peak, contraction, and recovery. Recognizing these cycles and understanding their impact on investment strategies can help you adapt and seize opportunities in different market conditions. For example, during a downturn, properties may be available at discounted prices, presenting potential opportunities for long-term investors.

Emerging Trends

Stay updated on emerging trends in the real estate industry. Sustainable and eco-friendly properties, co-living spaces, mixed-use developments, and technological advancements are examples of trends that can influence investment decisions. Assess the potential for growth and market demand in these emerging areas and consider whether they align with your investment goals.

In this chapter, we have explored the importance of choosing the right investment strategy by assessing personal goals, risk tolerance, and aligning them with suitable real estate approaches. By considering factors such as rental properties, fix-and-flip, REITs, and vacation rentals, you can select an investment strategy that aligns with your objectives and expertise. Additionally, understanding market conditions, conducting thorough research, and staying informed about trends and cycles will help you make informed investment decisions. Remember that investment strategies can evolve and adapt as your goals and market conditions change. In the subsequent chapters, we will explore further into finding and evaluating investment opportunities, financing choices, managing real estate investments, and navigating the legal and regulatory aspects of the real estate industry.

4 FINDING AND EVALUATING INVESTMENT OPPORTUNITIES

Finding suitable investment opportunities is a crucial step in the real estate investment process. In this chapter, we will examine effective strategies for identifying potential investment properties that align with your investment goals. By honing your skills in property sourcing and recognizing opportunities, you can set the stage for successful real estate ventures.

One of the first steps in finding investment opportunities is conducting thorough market research. Consider the following:

- **Identifying Locations with Growth Potential:** Look for areas with strong potential for economic growth, population growth, job opportunities, and infrastructure development. These elements combine to fuel a surge in rental demand and stimulate property appreciation.
- **Analyzing Market Trends:** Stay informed about market trends, including vacancy rates, rental yields, and future development plans. Understanding these factors can help you identify areas with favorable conditions for real estate investment.
- **Evaluating Economic Conditions:** Consider the economic stability and diversification of the region. Look for areas with

a diverse range (different types) of industry to reduce the risk of economic downturns affecting your investment.

Building a network of real estate professionals and industry experts can provide valuable insights and potential investment leads. Here is how to expand your network:

- **Real Estate Brokers:** Connect with experienced real estate brokers who specialize in the areas you are interested in. They can provide market insights, access to listings, and help negotiate deals on your behalf.
- **Investors and Industry Experts:** Attend real estate conferences, meetups, and networking events to connect with fellow investors and industry experts. Participate in meaningful conversations, exchange valuable experiences, and draw wisdom from individuals who have triumphed in their real estate endeavors.

Exploring off-market opportunities can be a fruitful strategy for finding investment properties. Off-market properties are not listed on public platforms and often have less competition. Consider the following approaches:

- **Personal Connections and Referrals:** Leverage your own connections and let them know you are actively looking for investment properties. Word-of-mouth referrals can lead to off-market opportunities.
- **Direct Contact:** Reach out to property owners directly and express your interest in purchasing their property. Some owners may consider selling if they receive a compelling offer or if they are motivated to sell quickly.

Once you have identified potential investment properties, it's crucial to conduct due diligence and thoroughly analyze the properties. Consider the following steps:

- **Property Inspection:** Conduct a thorough inspection of the property to assess its condition and identify any necessary repairs or renovations. Engage professional inspectors to evaluate the structural integrity, electrical and plumbing systems, and potential issues that may impact the value of the property.

- **Financial Analysis:** Analyze the financial aspects of the property to determine its potential profitability. Consider the following factors:

  - **Rental Income Potential:** Assess the potential rental income of the property by conducting thorough research on rental rates in the vicinity, taking into account essential factors such as property size, location, amenities, and market demand.
  - **Operating Expenses:** Calculate the property's operating expenses, encompassing property taxes, insurance, maintenance costs, property management fees, and utilities, to estimate the net income that the property can potentially generate. By carefully considering these factors, you can gain a clear understanding of the property's financial viability.
  - **Cash Flow Projections:** Calculate the property's cash flow projections by <u>deducting the operating expenses and debt service from the rental income</u>. Positive cash flow signifies that the property's income exceeds its expenses, demonstrating a favorable financial outcome. On the other hand, negative cash flow could indicate the possibility of facing financial difficulties related to the property. Understanding the cash flow dynamic is

essential for assessing the profitability and sustainability of your real estate investment.

- **Legal and Regulatory Considerations:** Ensure compliance with local laws, zoning regulations, building codes, and any other legal requirements. Consider the following:

  - **Property Titles and Ownership:** Review property titles and verify ownership to ensure a clear and marketable title. Engage legal professionals to conduct thorough title searches and address any potential legal issues.
  - **Permits and Approvals:** Confirm that the property has obtained all necessary permits and approvals for renovations or changes in land use. Non-compliance with local regulations can lead to fines or legal complications.

- **Calculating Returns and Assessing Profitability:** Assessing the potential returns and profitability of an investment property is crucial before making a purchase. Consider the following factors:

  - **Cash Flow Analysis:** Determine the property cash flow potential by analyzing the rental income and deducting operating expenses, debt service, and vacancy allowances. Calculate the net operating income (NOI) to understand the capacity of the property to generate consistent cash flow.
  - **Return on Investment (ROI):** Assess the potential return on investment by factoring in cash flow, property appreciation, and equity accumulation. Compare the ROI of different

investment opportunities to make informed decisions based on your investment goals.

- **Risk Assessment:** Assess the potential risks associated with the investment property to make informed decisions. Understanding and mitigating risks is a crucial aspect of successful real estate investing. Consider factors such as market volatility, tenant turnover, property damage, regulatory changes, and financing risks. By conducting a thorough risk analysis, you can develop strategies to minimize potential setbacks and safeguard your investment. Remember, being aware of the risks allows you to <u>proactively</u> address them and protect your real estate portfolio. Consider factors such as market volatility, tenant turnover, property management challenges, and/or potential unforeseen expenses. Mitigate risks through contingency plans, insurance coverage, and thorough property analyses.

In this chapter, we have explored the process of finding and evaluating investment opportunities applicable to real estate. By conducting market research, building a network, and exploring off-market properties, you will be able to identify potential investment opportunities that <u>connect with your own goals</u>. Through due diligence, property inspections, financial analysis, and legal considerations, you can assess the viability and profitability of investment properties. Furthermore, calculating returns, assessing cash flow, and understanding the associated risks will aid in making informed investment decisions. In the following chapters, we will delve deeper into financing options, property management strategies, and legal aspects to ensure a comprehensive understanding of the real estate investment landscape.

5 FINANCING AND MANAGING REAL ESTATE INVESTMENTS

Financing and effectively managing cash flow are vital aspects of real estate investments. In this chapter, we will explore strategies for securing funding, managing financial resources, and optimizing cash flow, to ensure the success and sustainability of your real estate ventures.

When it comes to financing your real estate investments, there are several options to consider:

- **Traditional Mortgages:** Explore different mortgage options offered by banks and financial institutions. Consider factors such as interest rates, loan terms, down payment requirements, and eligibility criteria. A traditional mortgage is a common choice for long-term investments, such as rental properties.
- **Private Lenders and Hard Money Loans:** Access alternative sources of funding, such as private lenders or hard money loans (short term loans from non-traditional lenders). These options may provide more flexible terms and faster approval processes, making them suitable for time-sensitive investment opportunities or situations where traditional financing may not be available.

In addition to traditional financing options, there are creative strategies you can employ to fund your real estate investments:

- **Seller Financing:** Negotiate with the property seller to arrange financing directly. This approach can offer more favorable terms, such as lower interest rates or flexible payment schedules, and may <u>reduce the requirements imposed by traditional lenders</u>.
- **Partnerships and Joint Ventures:** Collaborate with other investors to pool resources and share financial responsibilities. Partnering with individuals who bring complementary skills and resources can help you <u>access larger investment opportunities</u> and mitigate risks.

Managing cash flow is essential for the success of your real estate investments. Consider the following strategies:

- **Comprehensive Budgeting:** Develop a budget that accounts for income, expenses, and reserves. Ensure you have a clear understanding of all costs associated with the property, including mortgage payments, property taxes, insurance, maintenance, and property management fees.
- **Effective Rent Collection:** Implement efficient rent collection processes, such as online payment options, timely rent reminders, and clear lease agreements. Minimize late payments and tenant defaults to maintain a steady cash flow.
- **Expense Monitoring and Optimization:** Regularly review and monitor your property expenses to identify areas for optimization. Look for opportunities to reduce costs without compromising the quality of your property or tenant satisfaction.

Effective property management and maintenance play a vital role in optimizing the returns on your real estate investments. By implementing efficient management practices, you can ensure that your properties are well-maintained, tenants are satisfied, and rental income is consistently generated. This involves regular property inspections, prompt repairs and maintenance, effective tenant communication, and thorough financial record-keeping. By prioritizing these aspects, you can enhance the value of your properties, attract quality tenants, minimize vacancies, and ultimately maximize your investment returns. Proactive property management is key to long-term success in real estate. Consider the following strategies:

- **Property Management Systems:** Establish effective property management systems to streamline operations and ensure tenant satisfaction. Implement processes for rent collection, tenant screening, maintenance requests, lease agreements, and property inspections.
- **Outsourcing and Delegation:** Identify tasks that can be outsourced to professionals, such as property managers, accountants, or maintenance contractors. Delegating responsibilities to specialized individuals or teams can enhance efficiency and free up your time for strategic decision-making.
- **Maintenance and Upkeep:** Develop a proactive maintenance plan to preserve the value of your property. Conduct regular property inspections, schedule routine maintenance, and promptly address repairs and maintenance issues. Build relationships with reliable contractors who can provide timely and quality services.

Real estate investments come with inherent risks. It's crucial to implement strategies to mitigate risks and maximize returns. Consider the following:

- **Risk Management:** Identify potential risks associated with your real estate investments, such as market fluctuations, tenant defaults, or unforeseen property damage. Implement risk mitigation strategies, including comprehensive insurance coverage, contingency plans, and thorough due diligence during property acquisitions.
- **Real Estate Market Analysis:** Stay informed about market trends, economic indicators, and local factors that may impact

property values and rental demand. Conduct regular property evaluations and assess the performance of your investments to make informed decisions about adjustments to your portfolio.

To excel in the real estate investment landscape, invest in ongoing education and continuous improvement:

- **Ongoing Education:** Stay updated with industry best practices, market trends, and legal regulations. Expand your knowledge and gain valuable insights from industry experts by actively participating in seminars, workshops, and conferences. These events provide excellent opportunities to learn about the latest trends, strategies, and best practices in real estate investing. Engage in informative sessions led by experienced professionals, participate in panel discussions, and network with like-minded individuals who share your passion for real estate. By attending these educational events, you can enhance your understanding of the industry, stay updated on market developments, and expand your network of valuable contacts. Remember, continuous learning and staying connected with the real estate community are key to staying ahead in this dynamic and ever-evolving field.
- **Networking:** Build relationships with other investors and professionals in the real estate industry. Join local real estate associations, attend networking events, and participate in online communities to gain insights, share experiences, and learn from others.

In this chapter, we have explored the key aspects of financing and managing real estate investments. By securing funding through various options, managing cash flow effectively, and creating systems for property management and maintenance, you can ensure the success of your investments. Furthermore, by implementing risk mitigation strategies, staying informed about market conditions, and continuously educating yourself, you can maximize returns and navigate challenges in the real estate industry. In the upcoming chapters, we will dive deeper into legal considerations, tax implications, and strategies for expanding and diversifying your real estate portfolio.

6 NAVIGATING LEGAL AND REGULATORY ASPECTS

Navigating the legal and regulatory landscape is essential for real estate investors to ensure compliance, protect their investments, and maintain positive relationships with tenants and other stakeholders. In this chapter, we will explore key legal considerations in real estate and provide insights on how to navigate these aspects effectively.

Understanding property rights and legal ownership structures is crucial for real estate investors. Consider the following:

- **Ownership Structures:** Familiarize yourself with different ownership structures, such as sole ownership, partnerships, limited liability companies (LLCs), or trusts. Each structure has its advantages and considerations, so consult with legal professionals to determine the most suitable option for your circumstances.
- **Compliance and Transfer:** Comply with local regulations regarding property ownership and transfer. This may include conducting title searches, properly recording deeds, and fulfilling tax obligations associated with property transfers.

Understanding land use regulations and zoning ordinances is crucial to ensure proper use and development of properties. Consider the following:

- **Regulations and Permits:** Familiarize yourself with local regulations and obtain necessary permits and approvals for construction, renovations, or changes in property usage. Failure to comply with these regulations can lead to legal complications and penalties.
- **Consulting Professionals:** Work with professionals, such as land-use attorneys or zoning experts, to navigate complex land use and zoning requirements. They can help you understand and comply with regulations while maximizing the potential of your property.

Contracts and agreements play a significant role in real estate transactions and landlord-tenant relationships. Consider the following:

- **Importance of Written Contracts:** Understand the importance of written contracts and agreements in real estate transactions. These include purchase agreements, lease agreements, and contractor agreements. Working with legal professionals can help ensure that your contracts protect your rights and interests.
- **Comprehensive Lease Agreements:** Create comprehensive lease agreements that clearly define the rights and responsibilities of both landlords and tenants. Address important clauses, such as rent payment terms, maintenance responsibilities, lease duration, and provisions for early termination or lease renewal.
- **Tenant Rights and Fair Housing Laws:** Familiarize yourself with local and federal fair housing laws to ensure compliance and avoid discrimination. Understand tenant rights, including privacy, habitability, and protection against unfair eviction practices. Treat all tenants fairly and equally, regardless of their race, color, religion, sex, national origin, familial status, or disability.

Collaborating with professionals who specialize in real estate can help you navigate legal complexities and ensure compliance. Consider the following:

- **Real Estate Attorneys:** Work with experienced real estate attorneys to navigate legal complexities, review contracts, and obtain legal advice when needed. Seek their guidance on legal disputes, property transactions, or complex legal issues related to real estate.
- **Real Estate Agents and Brokers:** Partner with reputable real estate agents and brokers who possess deep knowledge of local markets, regulations, and industry practices. Leverage their expertise to facilitate property transactions, conduct market analysis, and negotiate deals.
- **Tax Professionals:** Engage tax professionals who specialize in real estate to navigate tax implications related to your investments. They can help you understand property taxes, capital gains taxes, and depreciation benefits. Staying compliant with tax laws and utilizing strategies to optimize tax efficiency is crucial for real estate investors.

In this chapter, we have explored the critical legal and regulatory aspects of real estate investments. By understanding real estate laws and regulations, dealing with contracts and leases, and working with professionals for legal compliance, you can protect your investments, maintain positive relationships with tenants, and mitigate legal risks. Real estate laws may vary by jurisdiction, so it is important to consult with legal professionals who specialize in real estate in your specific area. In the subsequent chapters, we will incorporate the understanding of tax considerations, strategies for expanding your real estate portfolio, and the importance of ongoing education and self-improvement as a real estate investor.

7 REAL ESTATE AS A PASSIVE INCOME STREAM

Real estate has long been recognized as a powerful wealth-building tool, offering the potential for both active and passive income streams. In this chapter, we will explore the concept of real estate as a passive income stream, focusing on rental properties for building long-term wealth.

Investing in rental properties offers several benefits; steady cash flow, potential property appreciation, and the ability to leverage financing. Consider the following:

- **Benefits of Rental Properties:** Rental properties provide a consistent income stream through rental payments from tenants. Additionally, properties have the potential to appreciate over time, building equity and increasing your overall wealth.
- **Property Types:** Explore different types of rental properties, such as single-family homes, multi-unit properties, or commercial properties. Assess their suitability based on your investment goals, market conditions, and personal preferences.

Passive real estate investing often involves hiring professional property management companies to handle day-to-day operations, tenant screening, rent collection, and property maintenance. Consider the following:

- **Role of Property Management:** Evaluate the role of property management in passive real estate investing. By delegating these responsibilities to professionals, you can reduce hands-on involvement and free up your time for other pursuits.
- **Benefits of Property Management:** Professional property managers have the expertise and resources to handle various aspects of property management efficiently. They can ensure tenant satisfaction, minimize vacancies, and address maintenance issues promptly.

Passive real estate investing allows you to leverage rental income to accumulate wealth over time. Consider the following strategies:

- **Mortgage Paydown:** As tenants pay rent, a portion of the income can be used to pay down the mortgage, thereby increasing your equity in the property.
- **Property Appreciation:** Over time, real estate properties have the potential to appreciate in value, further increasing your wealth. Market conditions and property location play a significant role in determining property appreciation.
- **Tax Benefits:** Real estate investments provide numerous tax advantages that can contribute to your overall financial success. These benefits include deductions for mortgage interest, property taxes, and depreciation. By leveraging these tax incentives, you can reduce your taxable income, increase your cash flow, and ultimately enhance the profitability of your real estate investments. Consult with tax professionals to understand and optimize the tax advantages associated with your investments.

In addition to rental properties, passive real estate investing can involve other vehicles such as Real Estate Investment Trusts (REITs) and syndications. Consider the following:

- **Real Estate Investment Trusts (REITs):** Real Estate Investment Trusts (REITs) are investment vehicles that provide individuals with the opportunity to invest in real estate assets through publicly traded companies. REITs offer a convenient and accessible way for investors to participate in the real estate market without the need for direct property ownership. By purchasing shares in a REIT, you can gain exposure to a diversified portfolio of real estate properties, such as residential, commercial, or industrial assets. This allows you to benefit from the income generated by these properties, as well as potential appreciation in the value of the underlying real estate holdings. REITs offer liquidity, professional management, and the potential for regular income distributions, making them an attractive option for those seeking to diversify their investment portfolio and participate in the real estate market.

- **Syndications:** Real estate syndications are a way for investors to collaborate and combine their resources to participate in larger-scale real estate projects. By pooling their funds, individuals can gain access to a broader range of investment opportunities that may be otherwise out of reach. This approach offers the advantage of diversification and scale, allowing investors to spread their risk across multiple properties or ventures. Moreover, investing through syndications can alleviate the burden of direct property management responsibilities, as professional syndicators handle the day-to-day operations on behalf of the investors. This enables individuals to benefit from the potential returns and income generated by the real estate investment without the need for extensive involvement in the management process. Real estate syndications offer a valuable avenue for individuals to leverage their resources, expand their investment horizons, and tap into the lucrative world of larger real estate projects.

Passive real estate investments offer several benefits that contribute to long-term wealth accumulation. Consider the following:

- **Diversification:** Including passive real estate investments in a diversified portfolio helps spread risk across different asset classes, reducing the impact of market fluctuations.

- **Passive Income Generation:** Passive real estate investments generate consistent cash flow without the need for active involvement or day-to-day management. This income can provide financial stability and supplement other income sources.

- **Scalability and Time Freedom:** Passive real estate investments offer the potential for scalability and the ability to grow your investment portfolio over time. As your portfolio expands, it can provide a source of income that offers financial independence and time freedom.

In this chapter, we have explored real estate as a passive income stream and its potential for building long-term wealth. By investing in rental properties, utilizing property management services, and leveraging the benefits of real estate investment trusts (REITs) and syndications, you can enjoy the benefits of passive income and accumulate wealth over time. Passive real estate investments provide an opportunity to diversify your investment portfolio, generate consistent income, and achieve financial independence. In the following chapters, we will set forth key topics and strategies for consideration concerning your real estate investment portfolio.

8 STRATEGIES FOR EXPANDING YOUR INVESTMENT PORTFOLIO

As you continue your real estate investment journey, expanding your investment portfolio becomes an exciting and rewarding endeavor. In this chapter, we will explore key strategies for expanding your real estate portfolio, including leveraging partnerships and networks to unlock growth opportunities.

Networking and developing relationships within the real estate industry is essential for expanding your investment portfolio. Consider the following:

- **Connecting with Fellow Investors:** Engage with fellow investors to share insights, experiences, and potential investment opportunities. Attend real estate meetups, conferences, and forums to connect with like-minded individuals.

- **Building Relationships with Real Estate Professionals:** Develop connections with real estate brokers, property managers, and other industry professionals. They can provide valuable market knowledge, access to off-market deals, and referrals for reliable contractors and service providers.

Joint ventures and syndications are powerful strategies for expanding your investment portfolio. Consider the following:

- **Joint Ventures:** Collaborate with like-minded investors to pool resources, knowledge, and experience. Joint ventures allow you to undertake larger-scale projects, tap into new markets, and diversify risk.
- **Syndications:** Engage in real estate syndications, where a group of investors combines their capital to participate in larger-scale commercial properties or development projects. Syndications provide a unique avenue to access investment opportunities that may exceed what you could achieve individually. By joining forces with like-minded investors, you can collectively pursue ventures that offer greater potential for growth and profitability. Through syndications, you not only benefit from shared resources and expertise but also gain exposure to a diversified portfolio of real estate assets. This collaborative approach allows you to leverage the collective strength of the group, tapping into projects that may be otherwise inaccessible or too complex to undertake alone. By participating in real estate syndications, you unlock the potential to maximize your investment returns and broaden your real estate investment horizons.

Expanding your investment portfolio requires overcoming challenges and embracing growth opportunities. Consider the following:

- **Market Research and Analysis:** Conduct thorough market research to identify emerging trends, growth areas, and investment opportunities. Stay informed about local economic factors, demographic shifts, and regulatory changes that may impact real estate markets.
- **Risk Management and Mitigation:** Continuously assess and mitigate risks associated with expanding your portfolio. Implement effective risk management strategies, such as diversifying property types and locations, maintaining adequate reserves, and conducting thorough due diligence.
- **Embracing Growth Opportunities:** Stay open to exploring new investment strategies and opportunities. Look for

undervalued properties, distressed sales, or off-market deals that have the potential for significant returns. Consider diversifying into commercial properties, development projects, or alternative real estate sectors.

Developing a comprehensive financing strategy is crucial for expanding your investment portfolio. Consider the following:

- **Financing Options:** Explore various financing options, such as private financing, refinancing existing properties, or utilizing equity from previous investments. Assess the best financing options based on your investment goals, risk tolerance, and market conditions.
- **Capital Management:** Implement effective capital management strategies to allocate resources efficiently. Monitor cash flow, maintain reserves for contingencies, and evaluate the optimal use of capital for acquisitions, property improvements, or portfolio diversification.

In this chapter, we have explored strategies for expanding your real estate investment portfolio. By leveraging partnerships and networks, embracing growth opportunities, conducting thorough market research, managing risks, and implementing effective financing and capital management strategies, you can navigate challenges and unlock the full potential of your real estate investments. Building a successful and diversified portfolio requires patience, continuous learning, and adaptability.

9 RECAP OF KEY POINTS AND TAKEAWAYS

Congratulations! You have reached the final chapter of "Real Estate is for Everyone!" Throughout this book, we have explored the vast potential of real estate as a wealth-building avenue accessible to individuals from all walks of life. Now, let's recap the key points and takeaways from our journey together.

Real estate offers a unique opportunity to generate both active and passive income, build equity, and achieve long-term wealth accumulation. It is a tangible asset that can provide stability, financial security, and a hedge against inflation.

Continuous learning and expanding your knowledge of real estate concepts, investment strategies, and market trends are crucial for success in this dynamic industry. By staying knowledgeable and remaining adaptable to changes, you can make informed decisions and seize the opportunities that arise.

By diversifying your real estate portfolio across various property types, locations, and investment strategies, you can effectively manage risks and improve the overall performance of your investments. By spreading your investments, you can reduce exposure to market fluctuations and potential downturns.

Establishing a solid financial foundation, that is, maintaining good credit and cultivating strong relationships with professionals in the industry, is <u>essential</u> for real estate success. By managing your finances responsibly and surrounding yourself with a knowledgeable team, you can navigate challenges and maximize your potential.

Now that you have gained valuable insights and knowledge about real estate, it is time to take action to embark on your <u>own</u> real estate journey. Knowledge alone is not enough; the <u>application</u> of that knowledge is what brings <u>real results</u>. Here are a few words of encouragement to get you started:

Start Small, Think Big:

Begin by taking small steps, such as investing in a single rental property or exploring real estate investment trusts (REITs). As you gain experience and confidence, gradually expand your portfolio, and pursue larger opportunities. Each step forward will build momentum and open doors to new possibilities.

Embrace Challenges and Learn from Failures:

Real estate investing is not without its challenges, but it's through facing and overcoming these challenges that we grow and learn. <u>Embrace failures</u> as valuable lessons. Then use them to refine your strategies and decision-making. With resilience and a growth mindset, you can turn setbacks into informed steppingstones.

Surround Yourself with a Supportive Network:

Seek out like-minded individuals, mentors, and professionals who can provide guidance, support, and inspiration on your real estate journey. Embrace collaboration, foster knowledge sharing, and harness the power of a robust network to amplify your success in the world of real estate. Together, you can navigate challenges, celebrate successes, and continuously <u>learn from one another</u>.

In closing, it is important to emphasize that real estate is truly for everyone. Regardless of your background, financial status, or experience, real estate provides an accessible and lucrative avenue for wealth creation. With dedication, perseverance, and a commitment to ongoing education, you can harness the power of real estate to achieve your financial goals and create a brighter future for yourself and your loved ones.

Remember, real estate can open the threshold to personal growth and challenging opportunities. So, take that first step! Move your feet into the stream of real estate. Embrace your own passion and determination and the knowledge that opened the door for you to experience the prosperous future of your dreams.

Thank you for joining me on this journey through "Real Estate is for Everyone!" May your real estate endeavors be fruitful, and may you experience the joy and fulfillment that comes with building wealth through this remarkable investment vehicle.

ABOUT THE AUTHOR

Dominic Lyon, a seasoned real estate investor, is a firm believer that Real Estate is for Everyone! As an owner of his own thriving real estate investment company, Dominic has established himself as a trusted figure in the industry. Holding licenses as a Real Estate Broker and a Real Estate Appraiser Trainee, he possesses a deep understanding of the multifaceted aspects of the real estate market.

Driven by his genuine desire to empower others, Dominic dedicates himself to assisting individuals in their real estate education and endeavors. His unwavering commitment to helping people achieve their real estate goals has made him a sought-after mentor and advisor. Passionate about fostering a strong real estate community, Dominic actively engages with like-minded professionals and enthusiasts, seeking opportunities to collaborate and share knowledge. His new project incorporates these ideals into it. www.hoosierrealestateinsider.com.

With his wealth of experience, astute insights, and personable approach, Dominic Lyon is a valued voice in the real estate world. Through his book, Real Estate is for Everyone!, he aims to demystify the industry, making it accessible to all and inspiring readers to embark on their own successful real estate journeys.

www.ingramcontent.com/pod-product-compliance
Lightning Source LLC
Chambersburg PA
CBHW060006300526
45794CB00003B/1105